poesy

The untold finally found its place,
in the form of her fluttering wings of poesy.

HANA ABDUL KAREEM

Dedication

to my father, whose eyes carried

my unbounded dreams

to my mother, whose love cradled

my unabashed worries

to my partner, whose words dissipated

my unflagging doubts

to my sisters, for their unclouded

constructive criticisms

to my soul sister, without whose guidance

I wouldn't have opened my wings to fly this high.

Contents

EN ROUTE THE REAL HOME 81

About the Author

Hana Abdul Kareem, a dentistry student at KMCT Dental College, Kerala, has been a passionate writer since childhood. She hails from Kannur and has completed her schooling at Darul Huda Islamic School, UAE.

She is fond of playing with words to weave hope, express various emotions to help herself and others cope, and remind one another about the ultimate purpose of life. Her poems take one on a giant wheel of merriment and melancholy revolving around the axis of a pulsating heart.

She plummets into the depths and soars towards the heights of fate whilst staying firm upon the faith that keeps one anchored.

Previously, she's written for many magazines and poetry compilations and has attained prizes in multiple writing, public speaking, and quiz competitions including the 'Proud to be an Indian' contest conducted by Asianet News.

Contact: hanahazza@gmail.com

Preface

"*In the name of God, The Most Beneficent,*
The Most Merciful"

Lips flutter about the words to utter

All mustered up in the corner of her heart.

The untold never made foes

as it was hidden in the deepest cells.

But the lost hopes didn't let it be,

the heart could no longer be a maze;

its horizons silently filled

with the clouds of her dreams.

The untold found its place

in the form of her fluttering wings of poesy.

Poetry for me has been a solace, an escape against life's mundane chores.

It has helped me delve deeper into the beauty of simple moments.

Poetry has been a creative outlet for me to rummage across topics, phases, feelings and complexities of emotions.

From the dreams I have been harbouring, to the words I have often left unsaid and to the conflicts within the heart that I find myself submerged in – the alchemy of poetry has always held my hands and guided me throughout.

Hana Abdul Kareem

Foreword

Her poesy, Our luxury

She captures the vibrance of her wings

and their restless urge to soar.

She lifts herself gracefully

yet remembers to return in humility

to be anchored to the ground, grateful for the Lord

above.

She weaves with her feathery pen,

dreams, longings and fulfillments too.

She carves out of crushing despair and nagging aches

too.

Her art stems from the sap of her poetic soul,

irrigated further by divine light,

a gift embraced by very few,

altogether forming a radiant, homogenous hue.

And so, with excitement to share the honor

of having been blessed to be her confidant,

now onto you, oh precious reader,

I welcome you to step into this wondrous world

with eyes wide and your heart bare.

You may walk in, shoulders crouched,

for the trials of life may have worn you out,

just as I did, having lost battles, I could no longer
count.

But I hope, pray and wish,

that as this ride concludes, you begin

to perceive the very gift of life

and all that constitutes it

under the soft glow of a gentle awe,

emitted by the sparks of her poetic flow.

Mariyam Thahira

Author, 'Earthen Po(e)t-ry'

POESY *is about Everything*

Perhaps one of the few rare collections that made me lose myself and occasionally even read aloud. Hana's craft is so solid when she brings all colours of human life alive through picturesque lines and animate phrases. Though she is a bit laconic in poems like 'Thoughts', Womb', 'Voids', etc. one would never fail to adore their spiritual beauty and dig deep into the insightful facts buried in them.

POESY is a glorious meditation that takes you through every facet of life and gives you this unusual experience of waking up out of a dream into reality. Every poem is free from tortuous language and Hana has skilfully smeared a mix of accuracy and care on each word of hers.

'Wonder' is the right word for POESY where it is too strong for anyone to resist. I am sure Hana has already found in herself a battle to be won.

POESY has made me incredibly proud to be one of her English teachers.

Abdunnoor Hudawi

Founder, LEXIS learning

Themes

Heart, A Home

The heart is a source of solace to its inhabitants. Here, the poetess allows ink to outline the borders of all that she holds dear. This section is a testament to the vivacity and power of love that flows from an untainted heart.

Hold Onto Hope

Only a soul that has tasted from the bitterness of despair and the depths of darkness can recognize the sweetness of hope. For, the light of hope is a beacon that paves the path ahead for seekers of ultimate success.

En route The Real Home

If death is the only certainty in life, why are we so averse to it? How does one lead a life with the realization of how death is lingering in proximity? What does it mean to live, knowing we shall one day cease to be?

HEART, A HOME

Thoughts

If only I could write

the way I thought;

ceaselessly,

fervently,

grievously,

with so much hope…

If only I could mould

my chaotic thoughts

into words

to write in raw ink

dipped in love

to spin poetry

in a faraway land

and pour it into

the vessels of the heart

so palpably alive.

Happiness

What if I told you,

happiness comes in various forms;

sometimes stitched to my dad's oversized shirts

laced with absolute love and care,

many a time my mom's honeycomb of a heart,

loving sweetly without any limits.

What if I told you,

they are the ones I house

within the sternum of my heart.

Womb

I'm blessed to have come
out of you;
the womb that carried me,
abiding by me,
with every inch of your being,
through the thick and thin.
An ocean of boundless love,
a sea of effortless care,
a river of immortal sacrifice,
a lake of endless affection.
No words could ever describe you,
the winsome lady of my life.

To all those strong mothers out there,
May we be them. May we raise them.

Father

His eyes carry

her aberrant dreams,

emboldening her

with every little glance.

Every other day,

he sews her a new hope

with his words,

giving her many ways to cope.

Always and in all ways

he was her raft

that kept her from sinking.

Beholder

In this world there is only you
whose heart like mine,
ceaselessly bleeds
in reddish hues.

So, rest your weighed down head
on my shoulder.
I shall be your beholder.

This pain was necessary, but dear,
even this is temporary.

When this feeling eats you
to the bone,
running through the skin
into the arteries and veins,
flooding your heart,
sighing for departure,

longing for the feeling of home,

dear, I shall be your home

when you no longer

want to roam.

My Better Half

If I were to confess about,

the aspect of our bond,

that breaks my heart the most,

it'd be the partings, the partings,

the partings.

Oh! how they plague me,

Oh! how they tear me from deep within.

After days of chaos and inner turmoil,

that moment when our hands locked,

creating euphoria with the shyness of your sleek smile,

I could feel the butterflies in my stomach,

with my each heartbeat echoing –

we are finally one.

Fits of your uninhibited laughter

creating an aura of unfiltered joy,

one of the many moments

which will always be cherished

and longed for.

Fragrant blossoms bloomed

within my heart,

under the warmth of your glance

which in no time turned into a garden,

with your scent drifting past,

with each passing second.

To you,

to the soul intertwined

with the intricacies of mine.

To our unparalleled bond,

to be garments to each other,

always and forevermore.

Moments

I envisage us sitting on the rooftop

staring at the night sky filled with stars

and the full moon glowing with all its glory.

I envisage me talking my heart out to you,

with you all ears.

I see your gleaming eyes absorbing the beautiful night sky,

a sight for sore eyes.

I envisage our conspiracy of silence then,

contemplating over the magnificence of the Creator.

I see your lips moving,

perhaps in the praise of our Exalted Lord.

I envisage a night like that,

with you by my side beneath the night sky,

nothing but simple moments filled

with grace and beauty is all I ask for,

to wrap you up in the fabric of my ceaseless love

and lace them with absolute care.

Aspirations

What must it be like;

to be the glimmer of hope

to someone

to be someone's secret prayer

in the last third of the night

to be the moon to someone's

night sky

to be the muse to someone's

poetry

to be the clarity amidst

the confusion

to be the laughter breaking

through sadness

to be the balm to someone's

bruised soul

to connect with someone

on a higher level;

transcending all the boundaries

of this fleeting world.

Pages

As I walk past the rows of books,

I find you,

tucked between the crinkled pages.

In the space between the words,

a part of you resides;

that's where my soul abides.

A Blotting Paper

She was like a blotting paper
doing everyone a favour,
soaking the sadness around
without rebound.
Little did she know,
reaching the brim of it all,
it would be difficult
to unload it all.

Betrayal

I loved you with every inch of my being
beyond the need of any feeling.
I embraced you with all my heart,
never thought you would depart
leaving me broken
and bruised.
My heart aches.
I can feel it break
as I grab my chest
and clench onto my skin.
My body is numb
as I hold back my tears.
I can't help but cry
brooding over
your gift
of suffering;
the gift of betrayal.

The Ache

I have spent all my nights

writing poems about you,

hoping my heart will

pour out empty

but the more I wrote,

the more I ached for you

to come and fill the void

of this raging heart.

You;

my forgotten self.

Love

You may fall in love

with a thousand creations,

building up your expectations

but you see,

only that love lasts;

the love for your Creator.

The Wait

I see the clouds

dawdle

in the sky

as they pass by.

I keep an eye

waiting for the rain

to come by.

I stand there

in vain

but I shall

not complain

for the clouds

will pour down again.

The Moon

In the darkened night,
I look up to you
gracefully bright
seldom your light
but a reflection,
serenely alight.

I look up to you
and see a majestic might
brightening a billion's night
thou seldom your light.

And thus, I owe you
a few thoughts
a gratitude
for being my glimmer of hope
teaching me of ways to cope.

I owe you

for abiding by my side

when it is dark,

cold and everything hides.

Moonlight

Thank you for peeking through the windows,

enlightening our hearts, one glance at a time,

infusing a layer of tranquility,

reminiscing the lullabies

that our grandparents would recite.

Lockdown

Winding down through the labyrinth of life,

here is where we reached –

huge walls around to be breached.

I can tell you plain,

staring at these windows of restrain,

a reflection of ourselves is what we gain.

And now,

maybe it was always about

the little things in life

how we cherished and loved these,

no matter how much in rife.

Perhaps like the human touch,

of which we cared less

and said nothing much.

And now,

I find myself longing

for a gentle touch;

a handshake,

a pat on the back,

an embracing hug.

Maybe, even a stupid smack.

This feeling bugs me to the bone,

lingering through the skin,

flooding my heart and beyond.

The way we showed love,

and much more;

the gentle,

the simple touch.

Take me Back

Take me back to the seashore

I won't really ask for more.

For once,

to hear the waves sing

to remind myself of everything

I once took for granted

with the skies painted

in hues of blue

slowly turning orange,

the waves hitting the core

of my soul.

For once,

take me back to the seashore.

Floods

I used to take lessons

from the rain

and how it falls

on the ground,

uncertain,

yet nourishing

a flourishing

for dry land.

But suddenly,

all turned to agony.

A hero turned villain,

soft trickles to brutal shrieks,

come havoc, come fear,

pierce these living hearts,

that is, if you managed to find any.

And so, sweeping away
the believing and unbelieving
with laughter akin to a monster,
rendering all, non-living.

The homeless and hungry,
their terrified screams.
This is the sound of broken dreams.

But the living rest,
aware that this is a test,
knit their limb and body
into a fabric of humanity
to carry this ailing community
out of a sea of humankind.
A sign on their heads saying,

'One of a kind.'

Hatred

I'm so sick and tired of everything

that's happening around.

I just can't keep my feet on the ground

since peace now can't be found.

I'm so sick and tired of the hate.

It's so much more than I can tolerate.

When the hate mongers are roaming free,

celebrating the fall of the innocent lives in glee.

I just can't keep my calm,

when my brothers and sisters are forced to flee,

just because they disagree

to the blasphemy of the ruthless kinds

having crossed all the lines,

by the people who have lost their minds.

Where is the equality when it comes to the minority?

When my brothers and sisters in faith are killed

and left homeless by the strong willed,

when their propagandas are fulfilled

and the poison of hatred is instilled.

But, stronger than ever we will rebuild

the homes and faiths of our brothers and sisters

with the aid of the ever so skilled.

For they plot and plan,

but the best of planners is the Almighty.

On People and Lives

To a new beginning or to a never happening reality?

Isn't it beautifully strange how we come across
different people in our lives by the decree of
the Almighty.

They just crash into our lives and slowly become a
part of us without us realizing much.

That unforeseen crash first slows down into a gentle
pace of growth in that accidental relationship –

purposefully seeping deeper and engraving upon the
creases of our palms.

Some just seep into our skins like those henna-
stained memories.

Others nestle their way into our hearts to build a
home there.

Our lives then, like the hues of red and orange

melt and coalesce into each other's skies

to form a stream of happiness
characterized by its exhilarating flow
before expanding into the boundlessness of an ocean
transforming into this indefinite and unconditional
bond.

And all of a sudden, the thunderbolts begin to reign
burying our ship into the darkness of inevitable
estrangement.
We then find ourselves carrying remnants of the
mighty beings we once were woefully back to the
shore.

And we realize we're no longer part of the ocean
but rather something that has been returned to the
land where we had begun the journey,
as if it's no longer a ride we had once embarked on
but this story we were enraptured by as a passerby.

We then find ourselves reclining there –
silently staring at the waves
that changed the course of our lives.

Mother

Your tender heart,

a nest woven with unconditional love never ceases
to amaze me.

How a yummylicious piece of snack suddenly
becomes something which you don't like to have,

when you sense that I'm craving for an extra piece,

how you would sacrifice anything and everything
just to keep me happy and safe,

how you would bring me fruits well-cut,

in a bowl, so I could eat them with ease,

how you would come to look after me every now
and then when I'm sick,

with your tired eyes in the midst of the night,

how you would cook me my favorite dishes when I
come back home,

how you would always have a box filled with snacks
and chocolates

which you have kept aside over the weeks in my absence,

how you would sense the agony and tiredness behind my voice and dial me every now and then just to make sure I'm doing better,

how you would pack everything so meticulously knowing my needs when I leave home,

how you would check on me bombarding with billions of questions,

hiding your apprehensions behind it all.

How you would wrap up the gift of your love in these subtle expressions,

how does one have so much love within, strong enough to collapse a mountain of worries?

How does one love so selflessly like a moonlight pulling a blanket over the sky, bright enough to lead you into the embrace of her everlasting love?

It takes sadness to know what happiness is, noise to appreciate silence

and absence to value presence, as cliche as it may sound,

aren't we all living an ironic life then?

Overshadowing the very essence of our real being.

How much will it really take for us to truly appreciate a lot of things which we have taken for granted ?

The realization that I myself have been too negligent and the observation that it's normalized and glorified in today's hustle culture have already been bothering me.

How are we supposed to honor and give back the love, the warmth, the care

that is being showered upon us by the most selfless and genuine being ever?

HOLD ONTO HOPE

A Dream

I wanted you so bad

and I tried so hard

but it's time for you to depart

and I'm falling apart.

You know,

it's pretty sad

because you were something I never had.

But with you, perhaps

it was the darkness in me

that was diminishing slowly –

to be replaced with such illuminating mercy

of which I never considered myself worthy.

Pain

When the pain
starts engulfing you,
spread it like a paper,
fold it duly into a boat,
and let it sail away
with that dismay.

Let it go

I always held onto things too tight,
even when it no longer felt right.
I was deeply smitten
but they say it's all written;
Destiny, it was called.
When things are not meant to stay,
let them fly away.

Voids

A small void settled

inside my chest

slowly expanding

to crush,

plaguing my heart.

I, then try

to comfort myself

weaving a web

of false hopes,

untangling my

thoughts in loops

lest my worries

come to naught.

Hold On

Dear self,

hold on a little longer

for the times you fought,

yet failed desolately,

for the words you left untold

and thoughts unvoiced,

for the feigned smiles

and implicit feelings,

for the erratic dreams

and esoteric aspirations,

hold on a little longer.

Whispers

Eyes cried

with sorrows buried

dabbling in darkness

melting away the sadness,

quieting my restive soul

and screaming heart.

I whispered,

"This too shall pass."

Dreams

I too had some dreams,

so adamant and alluring.

Those dreams would blend into reality,

I thought,

like a fulfilled fantasy.

How could I have foreseen the path ahead,

unbeknownst to me,

with those dreams sneaking off.

Maybe,

I should start dreaming again.

Bygones

When the bygone agony returns,

the heart inside me mourns

its blood,

brutally burns

with every beat.

I feel the heat,

the bitter defeat,

and hence, I ask

"Was it too soon to retreat?"

Strength

A soul split into a thousand emotions,

holding on to certain notions.

The mind spins and spins,

with hopeless thoughts in grins.

When your heart is weak,

strength is what you seek.

The Key

I walk

through the narrow aisles of pain

in search for the euphoric key

to unlock the ever melancholic heart.

Exhausted,

by the noise and silence,

the light and dark;

hope and despair.

Unfazed by the pain,

determined to make the gain.

Path

The path ahead seems so bleak,

my heart here is racing in murk.

Having locked up the ludic spirit within,

The person I long to be seems miles away.

All I see now are silhouettes,

life now seems like a labyrinth,

hope now seems like a set of letters

mustered up just to make a word.

My fragile heart;

a mirrored pool of words

brimful with inane thoughts.

Words yet to unfold,

like a whisper in the untamed wind.

I couldn't be the heroine of my dreams,

nor the care-taker of my abandoned hopes.

Hope

Hoping against hope,

searching for

the strength to cope.

Where are we lost?

you and I will be tested

but please don't get exhausted.

Hold onto faith's rope.

Don't just lose hope.

Surely, you can focus and cope.

Faith

Let faith be

your anchor

when the tumultuous waves

hit harder.

If the sailing

gets tougher,

don't give up

sooner.

For, it will get

smoother.

With your Lord

by your side,

things will get better.

Knots

In the thread of your heart,

I knotted

my knots of

unshed tears,

untold fears,

unbounded stories,

unabated worries,

unrequited love,

unwearied struggles

and unabashed dreams

pinning my hopes

on you

unknotting it

one by one

slowly but steadily.

You'll be Okay

I look at her

sunken eyes and swollen lips

with agony engraved on her face

tears flooding her eyes,

spilling down her cheeks.

A tightening of her throat,

a short intake of breath

robbing her of the ability to speak

as the grief poured out

in a gush of endless tears.

Wiping her face,

forcing herself to breathe steadily,

she mumbled,

"I'm okay".

The Race

When you teeter
and your faith begins to waver,
continue the race,
for everything
will soon fall into place.

When your heart is sore
and every inch of it throbs
seek solace in The Supreme
for surely, that will suffice.

Seasons

Hold on

through the stormy nights

for it's time to turn over a new leaf

to give your heart

every reason to grow

through every season.

And this too shall pass,

albeit rather slowly

this too shall pass,

and blot out wholly.

Strive

You stumbled and strived.

Be proud! you tried

This is part of the path,

You were David before Goliath.

Hey!

Stay strong,

even when things go wrong.

Take no Shame

All these miles covered

the pain suffered

all for the dreams,

you so dearly kindled.

Find your way into the light,

don't give up without a fight.

Take no shame

in not being the same,

for you are supposed

to be a whimsical claim.

Thrive

Survive the stirring storm,

let it be a reform.

Thrive inside them

and break through the gloom

to sink into the clouds

that drift into dreams.

Best Days

Maybe,
the best days of your life
haven't happened yet.
There are going to be days
that will bask you with all the love and warmth
making a way out to surmount
the darkness that you dwelled in.

There are going to be nights that will pass by
while you talk your heart out to your loved ones
amidst the company of sparkling stars.

There will be someone
that comes along one day
who will swoop you off your feet
like a knight in a shining armor.
There will come someone
who will build a home in your heart,
who will peep through the windows of your silence
to get a glimpse at your castle of words

and then gather it up to build
a bridge from their heart to yours.

There will come a day
when you will see
your prayers blending into a reality
like a fulfilled fantasy.

There will come a day when you will be completely
freed
from the yoke of materialism.

There will come a day
when you will be elevated
to a state of absolute contentment.

Until then, my dear,
keep believing.
keep trusting.
keep striving.
keep moving.
You're on your way.
You will get there sooner.

Prayers

When you feel the weight
of the world on your shoulders,
when your heart grows colder
in the warm light of the day
raise your hands up to the sky,
let the Lord of the heavens
hear your cry.

Solace

The umpteen thoughts I have to put up with every other day, nursing and harnessing all the negatives around,

only to go down like a lead balloon and go haywire.

'I can't even begin to fathom the depth of anguish I'm about to embark on

I don't know how I'm going to get through this phase

I think I'm going to mess up everything now'

Surprisingly or not, time and again the Almighty have gotten me through it all,

even when my hopes were dangling over a pit of abyss,

even when my ungrateful self left no stone unturned to create

the worst possible scenarios and a havoc within my fragile heart.

And whenever I feel awful and get into the verge of sabotaging myself,

I'm reminded about how the Almighty helped me through it all.

Oh! how they comfort me, bringing immense calm.

EN ROUTE THE REAL HOME

The Truth

You and I,

created from

a drop of sperm

ending up

as a rotting corpse

ceaseless hopers

of the world

with our

hearts hurled

whilst the truth

about death

is unfurled.

The Reality

Today,
I'm dressed in a
multi-hued garment
so alluring and appealing
of conceit and comfort
adorned by
desires and deficits.
But sooner,
I'll be dressed in a
milky-white garment
so unsightly and unappealing
of remorse and regret
adorned by
distress and disdain.

The Hereafter

The life with its brevity,

the death with its precipitancy

never ceases to amaze me.

Yet,

I only prepare for

the transience,

spurning the certitude.

What am I really scuffling for?

For an ephemeral world?

For the appetite of desires?

How does someone bring themselves

out of the constriction

of this world

into the expansion

of the Next World?

The Residents

O' future resident of the grave

What more do you crave?

Inevitable is the suffering of mortality,

for death is the ultimate reality.

If death strikes,

are we equipped and prepared for it?

What legacy are we leaving behind?

How many hearts have we touched?

Will our chests of good deeds suffice?

Are we ready for the meeting with the Almighty?

Deception

Sometimes,

like a raindrop

a word

a person

that's all it takes

to create a havoc,

to flood your heart,

to make it brimful

with malaise

like a malady

which affects

the deepest cells

of your heart.

In this world, where,

we are all engrossed

in husks rather than the pith,

after each passing day,

in the softest corners

of my heart

it reverberates louder

than ever.

Lest anyone forget,

this world is nothing

but an enjoyment

of deception.

A Fallacy

Amidst the crowd,

I am all alone.

Maybe, here is not

where I belong.

What's this world

but a fallacy,

delights with its fantasy

for a moment

then deprives of it in the next.

With the world spinning

in its own pace,

having fallen behind

in its treacherous race,

I am in search of a place

which I can embrace.

Despair

The despair growing like a weight
I can't carry anymore,
my mind now is a conveyor belt of apprehensions;
the state of my people,
the way we are progressing
and taking strides to absolute destruction,
the very thought is prodding me from within.
How I can only lay here in nonchalance
drifting into a momentarily mindless slumber,
seeing my people go further away from the right,
normalising everything that's wrong,
wallowing in sheer ignorance,
celebrating the downfall of our own existence.

Where will this tangled path
we are trudging through
lead us to
other than our own desolation?

It's high time we re-evaluate our priorities

and redirect our journeys

to ensure we succeed

in both worlds, eventually.

So that we can prevent

the loss we seem to seek,

and instead try to spread

goodness with our actions and speech.

Remembrance

You nourished my weary soul,

which then flourished

in your remembrance

etching a way out of every woe,

sketching the path to grow.

The Soul

I was nothing,
but a lump of flesh,
until you breathed
the *Rooh* into me.

The *Dunya*
deceived me.
I could be anything,
thought me.

Being indiscreet,
my *Nafs* –
in it, strolled.

Struck me, then,
a comet of truth.

I was nothing

but a lump of flesh

until you breathed

the *Rooh* into me.

*(Dunya – the temporal world and its earthly concerns
and possessions*

Rooh – the soul

Nafs – the self)

The Mirror

The mirror of my heart

has rusted

with dubiety.

It's encrusted.

Should it just be dusted?

For, nothing around

can be trusted,

except the words

of The Entrusted.

The Holy Month

You made me fall in love,

with sunsets as I quenched my thirst

and satiated my hunger

with a cup of water and a morsel of food.

Those sleepless nights

invoked a sense of joy

as I stood in praise of my Creator

obliterating much dross.

I found solace in reciting

the mighty words of the Almighty.

You have made me a better person,

a lot more patient, tolerant, kind and giving.

I will long for you,

looking forward to seeing you again.

(**Ramadan** is the ninth month of the Islamic calendar, observed by Muslims worldwide as a month of fasting (*sawm*), *prayer, reflection and community.*)

Pearly Gates

I heard descriptions of pearly gates
I can't help but think of what awaits
I don't know how much longer I have to wait
It will only take a simple twist of fate
by my Lord – The Great.

Paradise,
A beauty beyond our conception
without any form of deception
Fulfilling the sweetness of desire
with everything that hearts require.

Abundance of glory
for the eyes to delight in
Magnificent mansions
for the righteous to reside in.

The rivers of water, milk,
honey and wine that flows
Cleansing all flaws with undiluted purity,
preserving all the dignity.

An eternal abode with
boundless bounties,
made of gold and silver,
pearls and emeralds
Its soil of saffron,
with the fragrance of musk
engulfing the air.

No weariness shall overtake
the believers
for they were never
the deceivers.

The golden trunked trees
furnished with immense blessings
that doesn't cease
in the gardens of peace
for the believers who endured
the hardships with ease.

Acknowledgement

My utmost gratitude and praise is for the Almighty, for I know it is not my talent alone but what the Almighty has made easy for me to word.

There are not enough words that will help me string together a paragraph which can best describe how I want to appreciate all those who appreciated me all along. But this little dream of mine wouldn't have blended into a beautiful reality without the constant encouragement and support from my amazing family, friends, teachers and well-wishers.

My father, Abdul Kareem, who has been my armour and pillar of strength. Thank you, for instilling the love of reading in me right from my childhood days, for inspiring me to write and for always being my biggest cheerleader.

My mother, Shuhaiba, without whose undying support and prayers, I wouldn't have done any bit of this. Thank you for helping me flutter my wings in exploration of this vast world.

My beautiful sisters, Hazza, Amina and Hifza, my most cherished treasures, for being my constant critics, for looking up to me, for always keeping up with my inane talks.

My partner, Shahsad, you came to me like a cool wafting breeze, lending wings to my dreams, carrying me into a fanciful flight. For the blessing that you are, thank you for being my ardent listener, for always bearing up with my random poetry outbursts and for inspiring me in every possible way.

My soul sister, Mariyam Thahira, it amazes me how our friendship itself grew gradually but took roots so deep it's helped anchor our very souls against waves upon waves of this journey of life. This book wouldn't have been possible without you by my side with your valuable words, suggestions and edits, right from the beginning. I honestly couldn't have asked for more.

Abdunnoor Hudawi, who has been instrumental in guiding me throughout the process and for writing a great foreword for this book with so much detail and dedication.

I wish I could name a lot of people here but I'm afraid that will be a long list.

I will forever be grateful to all my family members, cousins, teachers, friends and well-wishers for contributing in my journey with their wholehearted support, encouraging words and divine prayers.

However, I would like to mention a few here for being a special source of inspiration for me.

Sabith, my uncle, for always thinking highly of me, my friends Jazeela, Aysha and Rishika for always keeping me grounded,

Mohammed, Mariyam, Shifna, Aysha, Jumana, Muhsin and Hamza for inspiring me to write more and for taking the time to read through and for sharing your valuable words and opinions.

If it weren't for the obstacle-strewn roads and eye opening experiences of life, I wouldn't have learned the lessons or found enough muse to pen about.

Last but not least, this acknowledgement would be incomplete without mentioning my Instagram family for helping me rise as a writer, as a budding poet, for being an open and encouraging platform to showcase my writings and to grow together.

and so, she dreamt on,

and wove them with love,

into poems and prose

evoking hope,

and reminding of home.